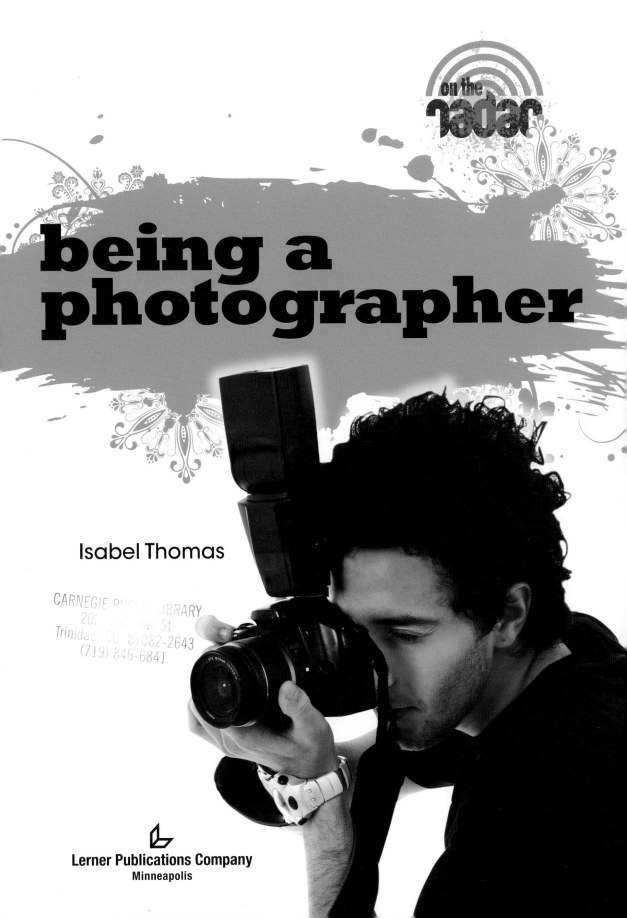

being a photographer

Isabel Thomas

Lerner Publications Company
Minneapolis

First American edition published in
2012 by Lerner Publishing Group, Inc.
Published by arrangement with
Wayland, a division of Hachette
Children's books

Copyright © Wayland 2012

Lerner Publications Company
A division of Lerner Publishing Group, Inc.
241 First Avenue North
Minneapolis, MN U.S.A.

Website address: www.lernerbooks.com

Library of Congress
Cataloging-in-Publication Data

Thomas, Isabel, 1980-
    Being a photographer / by Isabel Thomas.
       p.   cm. — (On the radar: awesome jobs)
    Includes index.
       ISBN 978-0-7613-7779-5 (lib. bdg. : alk. paper)
       1. Photography–Vocational guidance–Juvenile
literature. 2. Photographers–Juvenile literature. I. Title.
TR154.T56 2013
770.23—dc23   2011052671

Manufactured in the United States of America
 – CG – 7/15/12

Acknowledgments: Fotolia: Pavel Losevsky
6-7bg; Getty Images: 3r, 20-21; Alice Hawkins: 29;
iStockphoto: David Ahn 15br; Adam Lawrence:
26c, 27; Library of Congress: Lewis Wickes Hine 2b,
3r, Dorothea Lange 8l; National Archives: Ansel
Adams 9; Rex Features: Startraks Photo 22-23;
Shutterstock: Yuri Arcurs 4-5, Yan B 3l, 30-31,
BonD80 15tl, S Bukley 26l, Helga Esteb 25, 26r,
Featureflash 11, Iofoto cover, Mike Ledray 14b,
Left Eyed Photography 15bl, Nagy Melinda 2c, 24,
Sergey Mironov 14t, back cover, Northfoto 6bl, Joe
Seer 2t, 12-13, Jeff Thrower 15tr, Pedro Vidal 1; Kim
Watson: 16t, 16-17; Wikipedia: 20th Century Fox 10,
Robert Scoble 18.

Main body text set in
Helvetica Neue LT Std 13/15.5.
Typeface provided by Adobe Systems.

cover stories

the**people**

the**art**

the**talk**

IN THE FRAME

The lighting is set up, and the music on. The A-list actor strolls in, and I introduce myself. He is one of the biggest stars I've worked with to date, so the pressure is on to make sure the shoot goes well. I have just one hour to capture the shot before he is whisked off to the next stop in his packed schedule. It's all systems go!

Open up

I've heard that he hates having his picture taken, so I'm going to have to work hard to get him to relax in front of the camera. I make a few jokes and he laughs. I can tell that he looks more at ease, so I suggest we start taking some shots. I put on some music as I prepare my camera and other equipment. It always helps to keep the mood relaxed. Then I get to work taking the all-important photos.

Capture it

The photos I've taken are good, but I know they could be even better. I want to change the mood of the shoot, so I talk to the actor to explain my thinking. It's no good barking instructions like a drill sergeant at a celebrity! If you can get them to see your vision and work with you, it's the best way to capture a picture that everyone will remember.

Break the ice

Every few seconds, I glance at my digital display, checking the images as I take them. I tell him that he doesn't look his best in the shots and that I think we need to call in the stylists. He's shocked but then breaks into a huge grin. Famous people aren't used to being criticized, but I get the feeling this star prefers honesty. The stylists touch up his hair, and we're back on track.

The perfect moment

We enter the last few minutes of the shoot. Finally, my subject truly drops his guard and relaxes. Perfect. I adjust the lighting to match the mood in the studio. The ideal shots start to come, and I know I've hit the jackpot. For a few minutes, we're working together, and he poses for the shots like a professional model. When he leaves the room, I'm buzzing with adrenaline. I've got hours of editing ahead, working into the night, and a tough deadline to meet, but I know it will be worth it.

SHOOT SPEAK

Learn the lingo with our On the Radar guide!

call time
when a photo shoot is supposed to start

cast
the people who appear in a TV show, film, play, music video, or group photograph

crew
the people who work behind the scenes on a TV show, film, play, music video, or photo shoot

diffuse
to spread something out across a wide area. Diffused light is not concentrated on one area, so it is soft.

freelance
someone who is self-employed and works for different companies on short-term contracts

gofer
an assistant who runs simple errands

lens hood
a shade around a camera lens that stops light from entering the lens from the side to improve picture quality

light meter
a device used to tell the photographer how dark or light a subject is. The photographer uses it to set up a camera and flash correctly.

long lens
another word for telephoto lens. This lens on a camera allows the photographer to zoom in from a long distance.

paparazzi
photographers who take unposed pictures of celebrities, often without their permission

photojournalist
a photographer who takes pictures to illustrate news stories

Paparazzi often take images of famous people without their permission. Some stars, such as Brad Pitt *(above)*, request that the faces of their children be blurred if the image is published.

Photoshop
computer software that is used to edit digital photographs

portfolio
a collection of creative work, such as photographs, that are used to win new work. Portfolios are provided digitally, such as on a website or a CD

reflector
a white surface that reflects light back onto the subject

retouching
altering an image using computer software such as Photoshop; also known as airbrushing

roll (for backgrounds)
colored or white rolls of fabric or paper used as a backdrop behind the subject during a photo shoot

set
a made-up stage for a movie or photo shoot

SLR
single-lens reflex. This type of camera allows photographers to see exactly what they are about to shoot when they look through the viewfinder.

soft box
a box-shaped piece of fabric that is placed around a photographic light to diffuse the light and make it softer

still
an image taken from a series of images on a movie set

umbrella
a device that reflects light

viewfinder
a device on a camera that shows what will be within the frame of the picture

wrap time
when a photo shoot is supposed to end

zoom
to focus in on a subject to take a detailed shot

GLOSSARY

adrenaline
a hormone found in the human body that causes the heart to beat faster

A-lister
a very famous person

infamous
well known for something bad

press
newspapers and other print media

rapport
a close relationship in which the people understand each other's feelings or ideas and communicate well

MAKING A DIFFERENCE

Being a photographer is not all glam and glory. Some photographers—such as Dorothea Lange, Lewis Hine, and Arthur Rothstein—used their talents to document the hardships of people throughout the United States. Hine, for example, photographed children working in mills, mines, and factories in the early 1900s. He, Lange, and Rothstein took to the road to show what was happening in rural areas during the Great Depression (1929–1942). Lange's iconic images of migrant workers and the effects of the dust bowl are haunting and emotional.

Migrant Mother is the name of this image by Dorothea Lange, taken in 1936 in California. The woman in the picture is huddling in a tent, surrounded by her hungry children.

Lewis Hine's disturbing photos of child laborers—such as these boy miners in Pennsylvania in 1911—led to stricter labor laws for young people.

Wild beauty

Other photographers used the camera to show the glories of America's natural beauty. They wanted to ensure that the country's natural wonders were taken care of. People like William Henry Jackson and Ansel Adams went to great lengths— including parking their cameras in dangerous spots—to get the very best image. The pictures, particularly of Yellowstone, the Grand Tetons, and the Yosemite Valley, are breathtaking ... literally.

On the front line

Still other photographers took their cameras into battle, documenting the everyday life of U.S. soldiers beginning with the Civil War (1861–1865). Mathew Brady's team brought us in touch with the cruel reality of Americans fighting one another. Margaret Bourke-White was on the front line with soldiers in Europe in World War II (1939–1945) and in Asia during the Korean War (1950–1953).

Ansel Adams caught the majestic beauty of the Grand Tetons, with the Snake River in the foreground, in this 1942 image.

STAR MAKERS

The public's appetite for celebrity photographs began soon after cameras were invented. Since then, pictures have become an essential part of every star's career.

Before paparazzi, photographs of film stars, such as the legendary 1940s actress Rita Hayworth *(above)*, were taken only by professional photographers in studios.

Celebrity culture

In the 1920s and the 1930s, magazines such as *Life* were launched. They were filled with photographs of the famous and infamous. Hollywood film studios used glamorous portraits to promote new films, turning actors such as Rita Hayworth and Clark Gable into stars.

Fame sells

Early photographers used celebrity photos to attract new customers into their studios. In the nineteenth century, U.S. photographer Mathew Brady displayed pictures of famous people in his studio windows. People flocked to see the photographs, buy prints, and have their own portraits taken. Brady published the first book of celebrity portraits in 1850.

Snapping secrets

In the 1960s, some photojournalists—later called paparazzi—began focusing on celebrities' private lives. These photographers have captured many newsworthy moments, but they have also been criticized for the way they get outrageous pictures of stars.

A growing demand

The second half of the twentieth century saw an explosion in the number of magazines, newspapers, and TV channels. The rise of the Internet added to the number of ways people could access celebrity images. By the end of the century, celebrity photos were in high demand. Top celebrity photographers, such as Mario Testino, became as famous as the stars that posed for them.

With the explosion of celebrity culture in the 1990s, photographers such as Mario Testino (*below*) became celebrities in their own right.

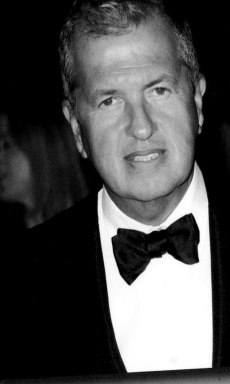

All change

Many stars only agree to be photographed when they have something to promote, such as a film, an album, or a perfume. Paparazzi photographers fill in the gaps. However, with the availability of high-quality digital and mobile phone cameras, fans can take photographs and upload them in seconds. In the twenty-first century, fans don't need paparazzi to get their fan fix.

Thousands of celebrity images appear in the media every day. Some are taken by professional photographers who are paid to capture famous faces on camera. Some people don't consider the paparazzi to be part of the profession.

SHOOTING STARS

On the red carpet

Photographers are invited to snap celebrities at events such as film premieres and parties. The pictures they take are bought by magazines and newspapers. Celebrities pose for the cameras in the hope that a great picture will appear in the press and help to promote their films, TV show, or books.

Perfect portraits

If celebrities are releasing a book or launching a product, they turn to a portrait photographer. These experts create beautiful photographs that can help to turn stars into icons.

Image control

Magazines hire professional photographers to take photographs of stars for their interview spreads. The shots are usually taken in a studio or on location. Top photographers are experts in giving image-conscious stars the direction they need during the shoot to create dazzling photographs that make great magazine viewing.

Being papped

Paparazzi take unposed shots, often without permission. They use special equipment and techniques to try to catch A-listers unawares, such as when they are driving or shopping. Some celebrities, such as Justin Bieber *(opposite)*, have fun with the photographers and photograph *them*!

EFFORTLESS COOLNESS

Finding fame

Successful portrait photographers are famous artists in their own right. They produce books and exhibitions of their work. Among the best are Annie Leibovitz, Mario Testino, Rankin, and David Bailey.

LIGHT WORK

After the camera, light is a photographer's most important tool. Special equipment is used to control the way light falls on a subject, from erasing hard shadows to creating the effect of sunlight in a studio.

A soft box is fixed around a light to diffuse the light and make it less harsh.

Styling shadows

The main light controls the angle of the shadows on the subject's face. Getting the shadows in the right place is important to emphasize a person's best features. Dark shadows create a dramatic image. A fill light, set up in a different position, can be used to lighten shadows and make the image look softer and prettier.

Flattering faces

Bare bulbs give out a harsh light, which may be perfect for a mean and moody look. When glamour is the aim, soft boxes and reflector umbrellas are used to soften the light. These tools diffuse light, by bouncing it off a larger surface or passing it through thin fabric. This gives shadows a softer edge.

Background lighting

A good photograph draws the eye to its subject, but that doesn't mean the photographer can forget about the background. This changes the mood of a photograph, making the image look more interesting. In the studio, photographers hang up large sheets of paper, cloth, or velvet for a smooth, seamless look. White or black are the most popular colors for portraits. These simple backgrounds can be lit up in many ways to produce hundreds of different effects.

A lens hood stops light from hitting the lens from the side, making colors look richer.

Reflector umbrellas and white backdrops help to reflect light.

Modern flash units can be tilted to direct the light toward a reflective surface.

A light meter measures the amount of light falling on a subject and helps the photographer decide which camera settings to use.

A laptop computer allows photographers to view their shots instantly and see if the lighting needs adjusting.

On a daylong shoot with photographer

KIM WATSON

FRIDAY

6 a.m. I get up nice and early for the shoot. This gives me time to check my gear. I normally pack my cameras, computer, cables, cards, and other equipment the night before. But it's always worth double-checking.

8 a.m. I arrive at the studio 30 minutes before the call time and meet my two assistants. I'm shooting the latest bridal and couture ranges by designer Bruce Oldfield. When the hair and makeup artists and the model Masha (in the photograph right) arrive, we eat breakfast.

9:30 a.m. We all sit down to discuss the looks and shots that we're after. As Masha starts two hours of hair and makeup, my assistants set up the lights. Our first job is to black out the studio because we need carefully controlled lighting. We're shooting against a white background, which should be straightforward. But I have to make sure we have enough definition between the white dress and the background.

11:30 a.m. Masha walks on set. Her whole look is breathtaking. There is always a feeling of excitement when a shoot first starts. I also feel nervous. I want everything to go smoothly.

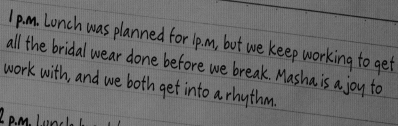

1 p.m. Lunch was planned for 1 p.m., but we keep working to get all the bridal wear done before we break. Masha is a joy to work with, and we both get into a rhythm.

2 p.m. Lunch break!

3 p.m. After lunch, we turn our attention to the couture. We're shooting against gray, and the look is more moody. My assistants change the lighting set while hair and makeup artists work their magic to create a bolder look. Our wrap time is supposed to be 6 p.m., so we all work hard to finish the shoot by then.

5:45 p.m. "It's a wrap!" I shout. I thank everyone for their hard work. As a surprise, the client has ordered some champagne for us and thanks us all for making the shoot a success.

6 p.m. While my assistants pack up everything, I sit down with the art director, and we go over the day's shots. We make a quick edit to get everyone's instant reactions.

9 p.m. By this point, I'm exhausted, and I head for home to relax. I have a couple of weeks to work on improving the photographs before sending them to the client. Once I've chosen the best shots, I'll send them to an expert retoucher to make my changes. At the same time, I'll ask the art director for his feedback to make sure that he is happy with the photographs before we finally show them to the client. Then it's fingers crossed that he loves the shots as much as we do!

ANNIE LEIBOVITZ

Living legend

THE STATS

Date of birth:
October 2, 1949
Born: Waterbury,
Connecticut
Lives: New York City
Job: Freelance
photographer

Leibovitz says of celebrities, "I am more interested in what they do than what they are." Her attitude and talent have made her one of the most popular celebrity photographers ever.

Discovering photography

While Annie was at college in the late 1960s, she took a trip to Japan and discovered that she loved taking photographs. She began taking evening classes to learn camera skills. In 1970 she sent some of her photographs to the new magazine *RollingStone*. The founder was impressed and commissioned Annie to photograph former Beatle John Lennon.

Radical rock images

Lennon's picture was on the cover of the January 21, 1971, issue. Annie began working as a freelance photographer and became *RollingStone's* chief photographer in 1973. She worked for the magazine for 10 years, shooting hundreds of pictures of music stars, including an amazing 142 covers!

Celebrity glamour

In 1983 Annie joined the staff of *Vanity Fair* magazine, where she became famous for her glamorous celebrity portraits. Rather than natural-looking shots, she prefers to take photographs using props and lighting to create striking scenes. She also persuades her subjects to do unusual or outrageous things. Her famous *Vanity Fair* images include actress Whoopi Goldberg lying in a bath of milk and actress Kate Winslet floating underwater.

Career highlights

1984 won the American Society of Magazine Photographers Photographer of the Year Award

1987 won Campaign of the Decade Award from Advertising Age magazine, for her American Express Portraits campaign

2000 awarded a Living Legend award by the Library of Congress

2005 the American Society of Magazine Editors named her covers as #1 (1981, John Lennon and Yoko Ono) and #2 (1991, Demi Moore) in a Top 40 list.

2009 won a Lifetime Achievement award from the International Center of Photography

Fame and fortune

Annie became the photographer of choice for the world's most famous and powerful figures. Her pictures also won her big advertising clients, who paid her up to $100,000 a day to create magical images. Annie combines magazine and advertising work and has a team of up to 30 assistants and stylists help her on every shoot. Her photographs have been exhibited at museums and galleries around the world. Annie is as famous as the many people she photographs. She is considered the most successful photographer in history.

MAKING DREAMS

Celebrity photographers don't always aim to capture reality. In this shoot, Leibovitz transformed singer Queen Latifah into the Disney character, Ursula.

Annie takes dozens of shots, so that she can choose the best one to create the final picture. She says that when she is working with talented actors, incredible images can be captured in just a few minutes.

A wind machine is used to move Queen Latifah's wig. It gives the final photos an active look, bringing the character to life.

Annie's assistants help to position the lighting props to get the right effect. The umbrella can be moved to diffuse light exactly where Annie needs it.

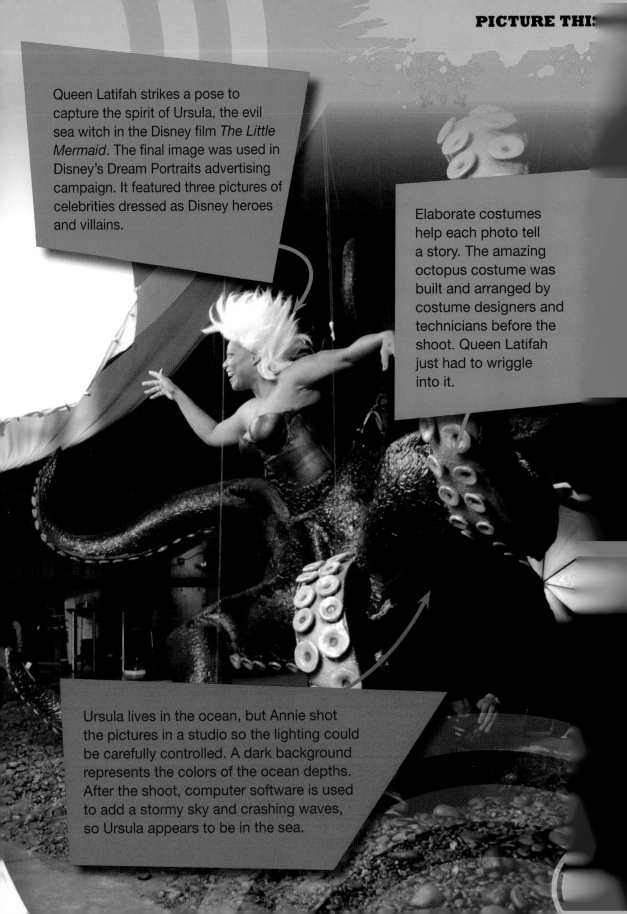

Queen Latifah strikes a pose to capture the spirit of Ursula, the evil sea witch in the Disney film *The Little Mermaid*. The final image was used in Disney's Dream Portraits advertising campaign. It featured three pictures of celebrities dressed as Disney heroes and villains.

Elaborate costumes help each photo tell a story. The amazing octopus costume was built and arranged by costume designers and technicians before the shoot. Queen Latifah just had to wriggle into it.

Ursula lives in the ocean, but Annie shot the pictures in a studio so the lighting could be carefully controlled. A dark background represents the colors of the ocean depths. After the shoot, computer software is used to add a stormy sky and crashing waves, so Ursula appears to be in the sea.

HELENA CHRISTENSEN

Model start

Helena is half Peruvian and half Danish. She grew up in Copenhagen and began modeling when she was nine years old. At 18, she was crowned Miss Denmark. Helena wanted to be a photographer, and she thought modeling would be a good way to travel the world taking photos. She moved to Paris, France, and then became one of the most famous supermodels of the 1980s and the 1990s.

THE STATS

Name: Helena Christensen

Date of birth: December 25, 1968

Lives: Copenhagen, Denmark, and New York City

Nationality: Danish

Job: Photographer, model, and boutique owner

Stepping behind the lens

For 15 years, Helena took her camera everywhere she went, building a large collection of beautiful pictures. Modeling for some of the world's leading fashion photographers taught her new tricks. She says that her modeling career gave her the perfect education to be a photographer. By watching expert photographers at work, she picked up their techniques and methods.

Shooting celebrities

In the 1990s, Helena used her contacts in fashion magazines and started to take on paid photography work. She shot magazine photographs and portraits of celebs and fellow models. Her experience as a model helped Helena get the best out of her subjects. In 1999 she helped to launch the fashion magazine *Nylon*, shooting film star Liv Tyler for the cover.

Going solo

In 2004 the first exhibition of her photography was held in London. Since then, her work has been shown in Amsterdam, the Netherlands, and New York. She has been published in the world's top magazines. Helena still models, but photography is her number one interest. She often shoots celebrity images for charity projects and has traveled to Nepal and Peru to take pictures for charity. She loves her new role as a photographer and says, "When you work behind the lens, you don't have to consider any limits."

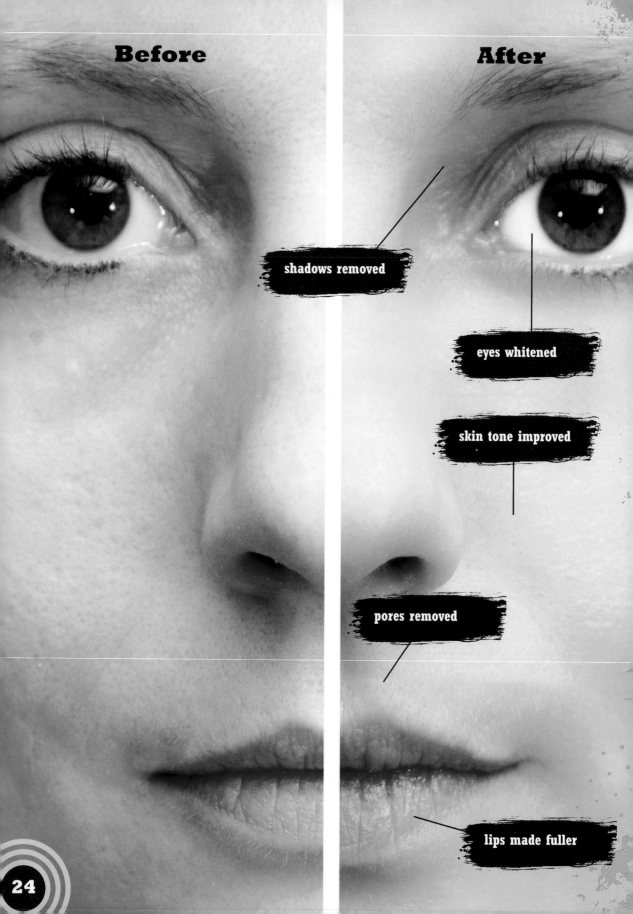

PERFECTION AND PAPARAZZI

One of the most controversial aspects of modern photography is the editing of digital images to erase errors such as blemishes and eye bags. Known as retouching, the technique can even be used to alter body shape.

Do images of celebrities such as Miley Cyrus *(right)* have to look perfect?

Faking it

The aim of retouching is to create pictures that people like to look at. In just one issue of *Vogue*, 107 advertisements, 36 fashion pictures, and the cover image were retouched. Standard retouching techniques include sharpening images to make them look clearer and improving the color quality.

Nothing new

Photographers argue that retouching is nothing new. Before computers were invented, flattering lighting, wide-angled lenses, and darkroom tricks were used to make stars look better in stills. The problem is that retouching software is so advanced that most photographs present images of perfect people.

Some celebrities are speaking out. Miley Cyrus wrote in her autobiography, "I'd see images of myself in magazines, and ... then I'd look in the mirror and see reality…. If you ever find yourself wishing you looked as good as Miley Cyrus ... just remember: *Miley Cyrus* doesn't look as good as Miley Cyrus in that photo!"

What the paps say

Paparazzi photographers argue that their photos are important because they are not retouched, so they show the stars in real ways. They also say they take pictures of people whom the public wants to see. And the stars put up with the paps because the celebrities want to stay in the public eye to increase their popularity.

ADAM LAWRENCE

On the Radar expert Adam Lawrence specializes in portrait, music, and advertising images. He has snapped celebrities and supermodels such as Jason Statham and Alexa Chung (*below right*).

How old were you when you got your first camera?

I was young, maybe seven or eight years old. My grandfather gave me a camera, and because of my height, I shot all my grown-up relatives from a low position looking up their nostrils!

How did you get into photography as a career?

When I was 20, I went to college to study Applied Photography, Film, and Television. I spent my summer vacations working as a general gofer (assistant) in a fashion photography studio.

When you are not behind the camera, what do you do?

A lot of time is spent retouching photos and getting the images ready for the client. I have to do photo shoot estimates, send my invoices, and keep my portfolio of work up to date.

How do you get the best out of celebrity subjects?

Celebrities, like Kelly Rowland (*below left*), are used to having their photographs taken. They can be a lot easier to work with than other people! I always tell celebs my ideas and ask if they have any thoughts about the shoot. It's important that they feel relaxed in my company.

What do you do if you have a difficult subject?

I try to make sure that everything is done as quickly and professionally as possible. Most of the time I keep cool!

Do you have any top tips?

Know your equipment! I'd say the most important thing of all is to make your clients feel at ease and build up a good rapport with them. The photography stuff comes second to that.

What are the best and worst parts of the job?

The uncertainty about when work is going to come is the hardest part of the job. However, working for myself is also the best part of the job, because I don't have to answer to anyone apart from my clients. I feel very lucky that I love what I do.

Do you have any advice for wannabe photographers?

You can start by taking a photography course at any age. But the most important thing is getting experience by assisting a professional photographer.

27

THE DREAM JOB

My story by Alice Hawkins

I was 14 when I decided to take a photography course and got my first SLR film camera. I went on to study graphic design in college, and after just a day's work experience with a professional photographer, I realized what a wonderful job it could be!

My big break came when someone from the style magazine *i-D* saw my work displayed at my end-of-degree show. He called me the next day and asked if I'd like to start shooting for the magazine. The following week, I was photographing celebrities at fashion parties! It was such a thrill to see my pictures published.

Since then, I've been commissioned to photograph dozens of celebrities including Gisele Bündchen, Kanye West, and Maggie Gyllenhaal. One of my best memories is photographing Elvis Presley's granddaughter Riley on a California ranch with a horse. I just couldn't get over the fact her granddad was Elvis—it was amazing!

When I get a great shot, I feel really happy and exhausted at the same time. I'm often running on adrenaline and staying up until the early hours of the morning looking through my pictures. Editing can be the hardest part of the job.

The best part of my job is photographing strangers from all walks of life and getting the best picture I possibly can. I also enjoy traveling. My dream is to photograph Dolly Parton. I adore her music and I adore her. I've been trying for years. I'm not going to give up!

SNAPPY STATS

$250

The average amount paid to paparazzi for a shot of an A-list celebrity.

26

George Eastman's age in 1881, when he set up his dry plate film company—the beginnings of Eastman Kodak.

1935

The year that photographers such as Dorothea Lange and Arthur Rothstein began to document the hardships of the Great Depression.

$250 THOUSAND

The average amount of money earned each year by celebrity photographers such as Mario Testino and Rankin.

$1.9 MILLION

The amount of money paid to photographer Annie Leibovitz in 2009 for her work for *Vanity Fair*.

$2.5 MILLION

The amount *People* magazine paid for photos from Kim Kardashian and Kris Humphries's 2011 wedding. The issue sold 1.5 million copies. The marriage lasted 72 days.

1975

The year Kodak scientist Steve Sasson built the first digital camera.

GET MORE INFO

Further Reading

Bidner, Jenni. *The Kid's Guide to Digital Photography*. New York: Sterling Publishing, 2011. This revised edition offers kids the latest ideas in shooting, saving, printing, and using digital images.

Buckley, Anne. *Photography*. Mankato, MN: Cherry Lake Publishing, 2008. This book gives background on the history, tools, and lifestyle of a professional photographer.

Ebert, Michael, and Sandra Abend. *Photography for Kids!: A Fun Guide to Digital Photography*. Kingston, MA: Rocky Nook, 2011. Read this book to discover how digital cameras work.

Leibovitz, Annie. *Annie Leibovitz at Work*. New York: Random House, 2008. This book features some of Leibovitz's most famous photographs. It also includes stories about shooting those photos.

Websites

International Center of Photography (ICP)
http://www.icp.org/
Head to this site to learn about classes and events offered by New York's International Center of Photography. It also has additional information about current and future exhibitions at the ICP's museum.

Queen Latifah as Ursula
http://disneyparks.disney.go.com /blog/2011/03/disney-parks-unveils- new-annie-leibovitz-disney-dream- portraits/
Check out how Leibovitz's makeover of Queen Latifah turned out.

INDEX